MW01113320

TO WAKE, TO RISE

TO WAKE, TO RISE

Meditations on Justice and Resilience

WILLIAM G. SINKFORD

EDITOR

SKINNER HOUSE BOOKS

BOSTON

www.skinnerhouse.org

Printed in the United States

Cover and text design by Suzanne Morgan
Cover photo by Edwin Andrade

print ISBN: 978-1-55896-803-5
eBook ISBN: 978-1-55896-804-2

6 5 4
30 29 28 27 26 25

Library of Congress Cataloging-in-Publication Data

Names: Sinkford, William, editor.
Title: To wake, to rise : meditations on justice and resilience / William G.
    Sinkford, editor.
Description: Boston : Skinner House Books, 2017.
Identifiers: LCCN 2017013584 (print) | LCCN 2017017331 (ebook) | ISBN
    9781558968042 | ISBN 9781558968035 (pbk. : alk. paper)
Subjects: LCSH: Social justice—Religious aspects—Unitarian Universalist Association—Meditations. | Resilience (Personality trait)—Religious
    aspects—Meditations.
Classification: LCC BX9856 (ebook) | LCC BX9856 .T6 2017 (print) | DDC
    261.8--dc23
LC record available at https://lccn.loc.gov/2017013584

This volume is dedicated to the authors of this book, who offer the sources of their own hope in difficult days and inspire us to discover or remember the hope and love that has never broken faith with us and never will.

And to Pauline Warfield Lewis, the religious educator at First Unitarian Church in Cincinnati, Ohio, who welcomed me into Unitarian Universalism in 1960. Mrs. Lewis was the only African American at the initial gathering of the Liberal Religious Educators Director's Association meeting in 1955. She inspired generations of young people by modeling a commitment to diverse community and to the blessings of pluralism, grounded in concrete and specific love and care for one another.

CONTENTS

PREFACE

Nineteenth-century Unitarian minister Theodore Parker proclaimed that ministers should preach with one hand holding the Bible and one hand holding the day's newspaper. The newspaper might be replaced today by a smartphone, receiving a 140-character tweet, but the point remains. We have always been a faith community with a spiritual center and a civic circumference.

We love to look back to our leadership in the great moral victories that have shaped our world: abolition, women's suffrage, and progress dismantling one legal oppression after another in more recent years. It was easy for us to believe that we were on a roll and that the arc of the universe would inevitably bend more and more toward justice. The Beloved Community was just around the corner.

The divisiveness of our times has proved that optimistic forecast very wrong. Just as followers of our faith and progressives in general were trying to take the next steps on race, climate change, income inequality, and gender identity, progress that we thought was secure has been called into question.

Our shock may be understandable. How could we have been so wrong? We find ourselves living in a world in which our assumptions about progress and truth and justice are not shared by so many of our neighbors. We thought the Kingdom was coming, but we've discovered that not everyone's heart is open to embrace it.

It is easy for us to forget that Theodore Parker preached in an era even more divided and divisive than our own. This time, at least, I hope a civil war will not be necessary to settle the course our culture will follow. We are not the first generation that has been called to insist that the way things are is not the way they need to be.

But the dangers of divisiveness are very real, and the divisiveness seems to be deepening. We have a long pull ahead of us as our faith calls us to resistance. Will we have the stamina to stay the course? Will we also be called to depth? Will we be able to put aside whatever innocence we might have claimed and engage with the real world that some of us are seeing now with fresh eyes?

It is so easy to dismiss those with whom we disagree as misguided, self-serving, or simply absurd. I find myself tempted to do that almost every day.

Our Universalist heritage will not let me go. I still believe, as deeply as I believe anything, that each and every one of us is a child of God, that the Spirit of Life moves even in those who would send us backward toward a lost Eden of prejudice and rigid notions of what is acceptable that crippled so many and took advantage of most.

It will take more than sound bites to point us toward the Beloved Community, even sound bites of which we approve.

The meditations, reflections, and prayers in this volume are resources to help sustain us. Far more than sound bites, these writings call us to depth and insist on truth. All of them can be read alone, to re-center and support our persistence. Most of them can also be read aloud in small group gatherings or in worship.

They do not simply present the vision of the Beloved Community—these times require clear eyes to see the brokenness around us. But they do remind us of what is most true and therefore most hopeful.

There is a belief in the African-American tradition, a statement of faith that says we can find "a way out of no way."

I hope you find, in these pages, inspiration to wake and to rise, so that we can support one another in living as if love were real even in these divided days, and by our living make it so.

Blessings.

Bill Sinkford

TO WAKE, TO RISE

BLUE TRIANGLE

I didn't look.
Like you, I didn't look.
I turned my head,
averted my eyes,
plugged my ears,
stilled my tongue,
believing if I waited
someone else would see,
someone else would hear,
someone else would speak,
because it all happened
to someone else.
I never understood
I would be
someone else someday
because I didn't
look like you.

MARTHA KIRBY CAPO

MORE LOVE: A CALL TO WORSHIP

We gather in community every Sunday in a state of conflict for our very souls—a state both expansively hopeful and restrictively confined.

We are hopeful that we might rise to meet a new day for those who seek and who serve the spirit, hopeful that each and every one of us might encounter the sacred within, among, and beyond every human soul, and hopeful that such an encounter might work through us to topple the idolatries of our age.

And yet we also gather as a people who are not yet free—a people confined, unfree, contained.

We are confined, unfree, contained because in this culture of division built upon the pain of the people at the margins, even the decent people hold our love too tightly.

Putting it in boxes, prefacing it with qualifications: I will love you if—I will see you if—I will bear the truth of my soul alongside you if—and only if . . .

You agree with me, you look like me, you stand like me, you think like me, you act like me, you sing like me, you wear your gender on your sleeve and produce it upon demand.

I will love you and will meet you in the sanctuary of our hearts—

If and only if . . .

You give me evidence of your good liberal virtues.

If and only if . . .

You never fail to speak the language of the movement and never weep upon a street corner out of grief for your sheer inadequacy and the vastness of the struggle that you cannot even name.

We are imprisoned by these ifs and these only-ifs. We are confined by the smallness of our loving even as our souls remind us that we can only get free if we all get free together.

And so today, as we intersect in honest work, let our hopefulness mingle with our conviction.

Let our willingness to love beyond our expectations or experience break down our long-held barriers.

Let our willingness to be honest about the hardest questions open us to new truths.

May there truly be more love,

With no labels

And no binary

And no preface

And no qualification

And no arithmetic

And no limit.

May there be more love to liberate us all, and may we keep on, today and every day, until we find it, and share it, inch by precious inch, with one another and the world.

NANCY MCDONALD LADD

3

THE COMMON GOOD

We breathe the common wind of the earth
no matter where we live, who we love,
what language we speak.

We drink the common water of the earth
no matter the color of our skin, how long we live,
the coverings we drape on our forms.

We follow the common paths of the earth
no matter our beliefs, how far we move from home,
the gold that we carry, or its lack.

May we live from these truths, our hearts
open to the holiness all around us,
our hands turned always toward the common good.

KATHLEEN McTIGUE

CHANGE MY HEART

My first year in seminary, I interned as a chaplain at the Denver Women's Prison, where on Friday nights we'd gather for worship. Which, I quickly learned, meant gathering around a CD player blasting what some call "Jesus-is-my-boyfriend" music.

The music would fill the room, and the women would sing along with all their hearts, raising their arms, filled with passion, swaying together, singing *Jesus, Jesus. . . .*

As for me—well, I stood in the back, my arms firmly crossed, hoping to demonstrate to all who might look my way, this was not my thing.

More than just feeling personally uncomfortable, I felt embarrassed for the women, and for all this cheesy superficial theology they had somehow embraced. And from this distanced and defended place, I watched.

So often we resist with our rational brains the experiences our hearts most crave. We talk ourselves out of the love that stands so close we could almost eat it up if we would just . . . stop. Let go. Love.

To receive love like *that* would mean an ongoing willingness to be *vulnerable*, an ongoing journey of transformation, breaking open and changing, being born and reborn again.

My stance in the back of the worship space was like my own little force field that had me *thinking* much about "systems of oppression, economic injustice, generational poverty," etc., etc., and therefore protecting me from any deeper engagement with the *life* in the room.

But then, between each worship service, the women would come and talk with me. And I started to get to know them, arms unfolded. I heard their stories—of greater loss than I could even fathom, more struggle than you'd think a single person could survive.

Then, Friday night would come again, and they'd sing. And they'd cry, and laugh together, and release from their bodies just a few of the stories I knew lived there.

One Friday night, I was standing there, and this song was playing, "Change my heart, O God. Make it ever true. Change my heart, O God, may I be like you." Suddenly, it just hit me.

I mean it hit me who should *really* be embarrassed in the room—and in case it's not clear, it wasn't the women singing and swaying. In that moment, it hit me, the words, they didn't matter. The theology—Jesus-as-my-boyfriend and Father-God-centered as it was—didn't matter. Because the room was filled with *life*, and there was just one person in the room who had failed to experience that life, embodied there in the fellowship of women singing about the possibility of healing and goodness and forgiveness and transformation.

And so, I started singing, "Change my heart, O God." I stepped in closer, and I started singing louder. "Make it ever true."

Okay, yes, I was still totally uncomfortable, but I was leaning into my discomfort, learning from it, letting it just *be*. Actually, it wasn't just uncomfortable, it was terrifying to let down my defenses like that, to invite these words into my mouth without clarifying what I did or did not *actually* believe, to sing with a full voice about Jesus, and how I believe in him and his love for me, how it saves me.

It was terrifying to give in to the experience, knowing I, too, had experienced pain and shame, beyond what I was willing or able to name. It was terrifying to just be present, in the midst of all that discomfort, in the midst of all that love. Terrifying, and transforming. After that night, I could receive more people more fully, be with more people more fully, love the world more fully, and receive love more fully.

Uncross your arms, lean all the way in. Love is everywhere.

GRETCHEN HALEY

POWERLINES

If you have ever
been desperate enough
to draw your finger
from your forehead
to your belly button and
then from your left shoulder
to your right breast—
you would understand
why they asked us to pray
for them on their journey
North.

The death that lives
within each of us seeks peace,
seeks gravel on our knees,
seeks company and lilies
laced around its neck.

We write their names in stones:
the ones that have been broken open in the desert
    storms,
the ones whose atoms have been tossed
like petals into a river.

We pray for them
in every step we take
toward our own mortality.

We know that God is in the journey
North.

DYLAN DEBELIS

I pull another basket of steaming dishes out of the dishwasher in our church basement. My partner in kitchen clean-up grabs a clean dish towel to dab the pools of water from the upturned soup bowls.

They ask, "So, what's your undergrad in?"

The conversations that happen in church kitchens are my absolute favorites. I have been washing dishes in church basements since I was eleven. Kitchen ministry fills my heart.

But not this time, not this conversation.

I know the look I'll get. I know they won't mean harm, but I can feel the shame creep from my heart to my face. I am staff here. They pay me a chunk from their operating budget to direct the ministry to and with their children and teens.

Surely I have a degree. Preferably a master's degree. Likely even a professional license of some kind, too.

"Actually, I don't. I didn't finish my undergrad." I turn to load the next round of soup bowls. And while I want to say, "I was close to a degree in child psych, if I move back to that state I'll finish up. . . ." But I just spray the bowls with the restaurant-style sprayer. Bits of barley and carrots fly everywhere. The conversation stops.

My eyes don't linger to see the raised eyebrows, the quick flash of judgment.

It's not that I didn't want to finish school. I just came from a working-class family where college visits and choosing the right school were a foreign world.

My high school teachers didn't see anything special in me. My brain functions more like a modern dance number done in the woods, upside down, than a neat and tidy ballet performance of *Swan Lake*. So I tumbled out of high school and headed where my friends went—to a big, public research institution that was all about third position with absolutely no woods.

It's not surprising I left early, feeling stupid.

I worked in what could have been the *Ms.* magazine top ten low-wage jobs for women until my Unitarian Universalist congregation needed a religious educator and I applied.

We were wildly successful, doubling the number of registered children and then doubling again. We won an award for growth and innovation and finally had to buy a church building to house our booming congregation.

I served on district and continental boards for my professional association, and my blog was often featured in the denominational magazine. But I never applied to be formally credentialed. How could I? I would have had to face the credentialing committee without any letters after my name.

My faith says all are welcome. My faith says we are all whole and holy and good. I myself have said this to dozens of children and teens. And yet, we have miles to go to make this so.

KARI KOPNICK

NOT ENOUGH CANDLES

There are not enough candles in the world.
Not if we lit one each time death came to knock,
for each man gunned down,
for each trans person attacked,
for each woman left battered,
for each child caught in the crossfire,
for every family starved by sanctions,
for every militant massacred.

If every time we gathered all together,
converging on town squares, green commons,
or in Internet chat rooms,
lit only by the faint dancing light of candles,
together lamenting,
together rejoicing the life that still lives.
There would not be enough candles.

At first, there would be runs on the stores to buy them.
A new practice taken up with vigor,
shelves left bare,
a determined remembrance for each departed.
At first.

After a while, though,
it would be just another item to buy on the grocery
    list.

Every night gathering together to read another set of
     names,
each night bleeding into the next.
And still not enough candles.

Part of me wishes that we would engage in this
     lament.
Part of me wishes those
who sell the guns,
and make the weapons,
and pass the policies,
and deploy the troops,
and utter racist words,
would all be there.

That slowly the names would smooth away
the rationalizations,
the false projections,
the twisted logic,
the false hopes,
the idealistic dreams,
that all dwell within the violence.
But I know,
there are not enough candles in the world.

SEAN NEIL-BARRON

PRAYER OF RECONCILIATION

We gather with a hunger for reconciliation.

What is done cannot be undone.
What is done next must now be done with care.

We gather because we are hopeful,
Because we have visions and dreams of a brighter
    future.

That there may be more than vision in this room,
These are the wounds we must heal together—
Grief and anger for all that has been lost,
Guilt or fear in the reliving,
Pain that has gone without sufficient comfort,
Mistrust that was earned, that continues burning still,

Every injury we may have named, and yet still carry,
Those we haven't, can't, or dare not speak aloud,
Those we are not ready to make public,
Those still not recognized, accepted, understood.

These are the wounds that seek replacement—
Not cancellation or denial,
Wounds we will tend cautiously,
Applying the salve of understanding,
Forming scars that mark our history,
Without disfiguring the future we might share.

This is not a time of quick solutions, fancy talking.
This is a slow precision. This is a prayer for peace.

We are new at this endeavor. New at listening, new at
    hearing.
New at taking enough time to honestly receive one
    another's stories.

What is done cannot be undone.
What is done next must now be done with care.

We gather because we are hopeful,
Because we have visions and dreams of a brighter
    future.

May the strength of this time together help us to
    walk forward.
May the wisdom of this experience help us to know
    our path.
May we have the courage to return, as often as neces-
    sary, until our way is clear.
May we have the perseverance, together, to see it
    through.

May we cause it to be so.

ANNE BARKER

WELCOME AND LISTEN

Though you have broken your vows a thousand times—come yet again, come. These words of Rumi speak to the welcome that is at the heart of Unitarian Universalism.

We seek to be a home for all who desire our company.

We seek to make a welcome for all those in search of our good news.

Come, come, little children, teens, young adults, adults, and elders. Come, families in great diversity.

Come to this loving home and safe harbor—but not to find a place to escape the world.

This is a community of engagement—and of creativity.

We come together to create boldly—dangerously.

We must create the Beloved Community with an awareness of how difficult it is—because it is hard work. It is work that challenges us to bring our whole selves and engage deeply and for the long haul.

Our faith, our tradition, must call us into community. Our task is to create spaces where we might know and value each other. I am here, like each of you, offering my life's story as a gift to Unitarian Universalism—as a gift to you—I offer my story as an African-American woman, as a mother of children of color, as a Unitarian Universalist religious educator.

When we welcome all our stories into the DNA of our faith we add value, richness, and depth. The inclusion of my story and all your stories expands the vision of who we are and what we can become. To be the Beloved Community, we must know that we care for each other as beloveds—not merely in the abstract but in the particular and the personal.

Wanderer, worshipper, loving of leaving—can we share our stories of pain and joy, memory and hope? Can we be beloved to one another?

So often, we are hurt and hurting when we get to the door. We need to forgive ourselves and each other in order to go forward into deeper relationship. Maybe some people cannot even walk through the door until there is first an acknowledgment of the need to say a word of forgiveness—forgiveness almost at first meeting. Our isolation from one another may be so great—our individual and ancestral pain so deep—as to cry out for reconciliation from the start.

And this reconciliation is something else that begins with listening. We must listen to our stories. To reconcile, we need to make peace with the past, not by ignoring it but by looking at it clearly from many sides, and then to move into renewed relationship. We must gain and grow from our knowledge of each other.

We have all experienced times of pain, grief, and conflict that have separated us. We all need to be reconciled with something or someone. Here in our faith we can try to forgive when forgiveness is possible.

Our ears open to hear each other's voices.

Our eyes ready to see each other clearly.

Our hearts enlarged to hold each other's pain and joy.

Our arms entwined in embrace as we journey.

Don't give up—don't stop listening to one another.

NATALIE MAXWELL FENIMORE

MY HOUSE

My house is not white
Nor is it built for men only.
My house is not a symbol or a surrogate,
But a home and a place to dine
On the loaves of different hearts and minds
Broken only to be shared by many
Instead of being hoarded by one.
My house is where
I drink deeply of red wine
That flows like blood
Not spilled but transfused through human kind.
My house is the holy communion
Of humanity and love.

ADAM LAWRENCE DYER

FAITHLESS WORKS

They say faith without works is dead
So I worked for equality
Next to my queer friends who wanted to get married
And I worked for religious freedom
Next to my Muslim friends who were accused of
    being terrorists
And I worked for racial justice
Next to my Black friends whose lives were affected by
    police brutality

Yet I didn't feel fully alive even after working myself
    to death
Until I let my work become a spiritual practice
Until I let go of my attachment to the outcome
Until I stopped chasing after political issues, one
    after another
I still believe faith without works is dead
But works without faith is just as lifeless

JONIPHER KWONG

There is a narrative of fear and decline that threads its way through the talk by self-described environmentalists. That narrative should be familiar to those who have studied Jewish and Christian teachings. It is the Eden story. The story of disobedience, a fall from grace, the loss of paradise.

The earth speaks, softly, of something else.

When I find myself on the lakeshore of Chicago, heading back homeward after a run, I see the movement of migrant songbirds in the swaths of goldenrod. They holed up for a few days while the hurricane hugged the eastern shore, and now they are tracking south again, tiny, ravenous, ahead of what is forecast to be a hard winter.

Dried scat from a coyote reminds me that the denizens of this concrete revetment are mostly nonhuman in the nighttime hours, when the cars go still and the only constant is Lake Michigan lapping the breakwater.

Three years ago the lake was at its lowest point in decades and we despaired of it. Have we moved beyond what is repairable? Has our hubris gone too far? Has our tendency toward sin destroyed all that is good around us?

This year, with the rains and the snowpack, with two years of extensive ice cover in the books, and another predicted, the lake is at a new high. Near the shore, some fish or other is running, my untalented human nose informs me, but from the tap at home this water flows sweet.

Resilience is something natural systems have. It is a function of the meeting of many, the combination of a multitude of properties, which together create further emergent characteristics. It is the ability of the coyote, an animal that evolved in the high plains to walk on desert or soil and dine on voles and field mice, to adapt itself so well to our city that it has become a new front in the urban war on rats. Thousands of them share this place with us, mostly unseen. One showed up in the freezer room of a downtown sub shop a few years back. But she regretted her decision almost instantly, and was caught and released back into the forest preserves.

They have adapted to us, and now we are adapting to them. We do not adapt as readily as they because we think too much, and we see symbols and long-term processes, while they smell what is in the air today, and whether there are mice or a cold snap coming.

There are times for lamentation. I have spent decades now working for a better human relationship with the non-human life around us, and I know the data better than most. In the course of that work I found myself a guest, a speaker, a preacher, a cheerleader, in hundreds if not thousands of communities of worship, Unitarian Universalist and otherwise. The people there humbled me. They, too, are resilient: faithful, hopeful, patient beyond my imagining, gracious in welcome, joyous in song.

Our desire to know has taken us down a long road, and we have done a great deal of damage. That is part of our burden. We have not reached the end of our ability to love this place, nor to solve problems that our earlier solutions created. We are not yet at the final ebb of our own resilience. The non-human —the asters, the fish, the four-leggeds—have not reached the end of theirs.

CLARE BUTTERFIELD

A GOSPEL CHORUS

The Gospel speaks
to hope rising up
from suffering.
In the music, we are not alone.
Each of our struggles is joined.
A congregation of voices shares
a battle with cancer,
the loss of a parent,
the struggles of a child,
the massacre of children.

From the depths of pain
we look toward joy,
toward gratitude,
toward what we find
worthy of praise.
In the church where
my mother took me as a child,
we sang Let My People Go.
I loved the singing.

For the Beauty of the Earth,
my father took us hiking.
I seemed to prefer his cathedrals,
the mountains, where always
I could see light shining through
the cycles of our days.

We sang as we climbed.
I hear our imperative
to go down and tell old Pharaoh,
with all of our voices.

For no matter how desperate
our situation, how deep
our debt, how grievous
our loss, how hateful
our transgressions,
we can always find something
praiseworthy, something
to make us grateful,
some glimmer of hope,
some promise of joy.
That is the good news
we sing.

MAURY ELDRIDGE

Most are unaware of this, but when people were being arrested and sent off to death camps, Hitler intervened to protect his former commanding officer, who was Jewish. People who hate classes of people seem to have little trouble liking and even being friends with members of that class whom they personally know.

They say familiarity breeds contempt. And sometimes that's true. My preferred expression is, "No man is a hero to his valet." So, getting to know one another isn't a universal panacea. But it also reveals connections, and with those connections empathy, and if one isn't careful, friendship.

And lord knows what happens if our circle of friends gets too wide. Not that this really appears to be much of a danger. I read that we in the United States are increasingly living our lives among people ever more like us. The myth of ours being a classless society is turning out to be less an aspiration and more a lie. In the political realm, people who align with the Democratic Party tend to live together in the same areas, as do those who align with the Republican Party. And how many people of another race live in your neighborhood?

I'm not pretending to be above the fray. On Facebook, the vast majority of my some thirty-five-hundred-odd "friends" falls roughly into the same part of the political spectrum as I do. I rarely solicit friendship among those with whom I have strong political disagreements, and do feel the urge to defriend following certain postings about health care or immigration or climate change—I find it extremely hard not to see disagreement here as about people's motives and character.

But, and this is the critical part, I'm willing to forgive those whom I've come to have a relationship with. No, this doesn't mean you have to be friends with every lunatic who appears in front of you. Although there is some kind of "but" that I hope we find when the impulse to cut someone off arises. It may be necessary. But.

Familiarity is a dangerous thing. But not knowing others is even more dangerous. So, what to do about it?

Chris Rock once observed that there have been changes in how people relate across race. He said most black people have many white friends. And most white people have one black friend.

If you laughed or just chuckled, there's something inside that suggests one really isn't enough. Hitler's one small act was hardly enough. To say the least.

But. Clearly we need to push some boundaries here. A little transgression might be a good thing. In these dangerous times, pushing boundaries might be all that saves us.

Knowing the other might reveal all sorts of things. About the other. About ourselves.

JAMES FORD

I PRAY THIS DAY FOR THE COURAGE TO BE . . .

The courage to be humble in the face
of inequity and pain,
to know that the power has been given me
to make a difference,
although not to end all suffering
or to save all the whales that populate our days.

I pray for the courage of endurance,
to keep acting in the midst of despair,
to keep trying in the aftermath of failure,
to keep hoping in the emptiness
that follows loss or change.

May courage give me patience
and may I ever know Love's healing presence
at the heart and center of my days.

MAUREEN KILLORAN

AFTER THE SHOOTINGS: A PRAYER

Spirit of life,

Help us. Following another week of brutal shootings by police of black men, then a sniper shooting twelve uniformed officers and killing five, we are a nation in mourning, a nation full of rage, a nation filled with pain and grief, a nation confused and on the brink of being anesthetized by the toxicity of race hatred. Help us.

Help us to find our way through the turmoil that turns people against each other instead of turning toward each other in love. Help us to see that little good ever comes out of viewing each other as the "other." Only when we find our common humanity can we co-exist peacefully and with lovingkindness.

As exasperated as we may become, we go on. The future beckons us to come to it bearing a faith and resolve "that passes all understanding." Like the birds of the air that can't help but sing their morning songs, we too, have a song. We sing of love, forgiveness, grace, mercy, compassion, friendship, care, trust, and the ability to transcend our circumstances.

We ask this prayer in the name of all persons present and absent, remembered and forgotten, known and unknown.

Amen, ashe, and may it be so.

XOLANI KACELA

PEACE: A MEDITATION THROUGH THE CHAKRAS

Peace resides at my root,
my ground, my rock of stability.
Peace resides at my core,
the coil of my energy, my hopes.
Peace resides at the seat of my will,
there is nothing to impede me,
there is nothing to make me waver.
Peace resides in my heart,
the crystal rose therein pure and pulsing,
the realm of love, in me, complete.
Peace resides in my voice,
calmness spoken reveals my serenity.
Peace resides in my Divine Eye,
my connection with the All, open and awake.
Peace resides in my mind,
the crown of my personal Divinity,
bearing the jewel of unity with all humankind
my scepter, my power,
returned to my hand for me to wield alone.
Restored, I go to work the ancient magic.
Renewed, I go to direct my power where I will.
Thus cleansed, I bring my peace to the world.

MARCIA TUCKER

FROM ALLY TO ADVOCATE

Thought I was so smart
Till I didn't know the answer
To why evil exists in the world

Thought I was so enlightened
Till I discovered comfort
In darkness for a while

Thought I was so liberal
Till my good intentions
Produced the opposite results

Thought I was colorblind
Till my eyes began to see
Differences that should be honored

Thought I was an ally
When what was called for
Was an advocate instead

JONIPHER KWONG

WHEN WE PAUSE TO REMEMBER . . .

When we pause to remember who we are:
    companions on this grand experiment called life,
when we take a moment to shed the ways we have
    been carefully taught:
to lead from fear . . . to punish the poor . . . to
    persecute
those who don't look like we do . . . to deny rights to
    those who love . . .
to believe that we are separate . . . that some people
are superior to others . . .

When we take a moment to shed all of that
and hear our stories
        hear and see each other into existence, into
    community,
when we take a moment to embrace . . . to practice a
    different way of being . . .

When we answer the call of love,
then we are living into the promise
        of building the world we dream about.

It is beautiful to dream . . . to cast a vision . . . to
    stretch our
minds into the future and imagine what may be if we
    were to

build a new way of being—not some day
but beginning again today
    beginning again every day that we have breath
taking courage with these hands and hearts
to make real the dream of a more equitable world . . .
to journey together . . . seeking to be transformed,
even as we transform.

Becoming explorers and learners in this world
    around us,
humbled by what we do not yet know,
fulfilling the promise of healing a fragmented world,
laboring not just in hope . . . but also in Love.

In this spirit, we commit.
In this spirit, we gather.
In this spirit, we pray.

ALICIA FORDE

Let me suggest an image: a table—a long table where people gather to eat. It doesn't have to be fancy with expensive china and chandeliers hanging above. In fact, it's better to be less imposing. Maybe a picnic table outdoors on a warm day.

When I was growing up in central Illinois, we often had summer dinners outside. It gets hot in that part of the country, and we didn't have air conditioning. By the approach of evening, the day's heat was still trapped inside the house, but outside, cooling breezes began to set in. My mother and father, sister and I, and my grandmother, who lived upstairs, gathered at the picnic table outside for dinner.

Dinners outside were different. The air was fresher, you could breathe deeply, conversation came more easily, and it often continued after the food was gone. We could relax, be ourselves.

Usually it was just the five of us at the picnic table for dinner, but sometimes there were visitors: relatives, a friend, someone new to town who my parents thought to invite. To accommodate them we brought out more tables and set them in a row. On one such occasion, a visiting relative from Germany had his first encounter with watermelon. He exclaimed in surprise, "I have never tasted anything so wet!"

What I'm envisioning for this imaginary meal is a table with plenty of room. We'll set places for each person we expect to join us. And we'll put out a few extra place settings for others who might arrive unannounced, without an invitation, whose names might not appear on the guest list. Isn't that a little frightening, to include strangers who might be disruptive or dangerous or might not share our social graces?

Well, yes, it can be uncomfortable: strangers at our table. In our lives today, we are taught to fear strangers. Turn on the TV or the online news or read the paper: strangers blow up airplanes, compete with us for jobs, steal our money and our identities. We devote considerable energy to protecting ourselves from those who aren't like us. So here we're welcoming them to our table?

But this is *radical* hospitality, hospitality that returns us to the roots. And the roots of hospitality involve not just inviting friends and family—not just those who share our outlook and values—but also strangers, outcasts. In the Christian story, Jesus was accused of inviting people from the margins to his table: sinners, tax collectors, those who would normally not be welcome at a dinner party.

In radical hospitality, we greet the stranger, we invite them into our lives, even though it can be uncomfortable. We honor that person's worth and dignity—and our own, as we open ourselves to who they are, what their stories are, how life looks through their eyes. We stretch ourselves to accommodate this stranger's view of the world.

As leaders, we offer hospitality, even to strangers we do not fully understand. Even the stranger deserves to be heard, has value, receives welcome.

BRUCE T. MARSHALL

ABIDING ANGER

I need a fishbowl where I can bracket hope for a
    while
I need a container to let my grief fill the cup before I
    pour it out
I need to feel the pain, the sorrow, the crushing of
    my soul
From racism, sexism, heterosexism, capitalism
I need to be in touch with raw anger
I need to weep until my eyes become bloated
I need to stay awake at night, sleepless from the rage
    inside me
Don't get me to hope just yet
Let me abide for a while with my Holy Lamentation

JONIPHER KWONG

CONNECTING

I'm white space
between black dots.
I grew up catching tigers
by the toe. School books
came with unbroken backs.

No one ever called my people X.
Families on TV looked like mine.
I burn in the sun. I believed
money could get me where I wanted to go.

I own the land I live on.
I was never a melting anything—
fondue, chocolate, molten pot,
hot lava lamp, or zombie brain.

A bubble surrounds me,
shimmer-soap surprise
I thought would never pop
until it did.

TRICIA KNOLL

"Walk ahead and let me put my steps in your steps,"
she said as we grouped to go up the mountain. "You
seem so sure-footed and I so surely am not."

It's from my ancestors, this sense I discovered as a
child, this way my feet can grasp the earth, can know
footholds on unfamiliar ground, unafraid. One
moonless night, I was eleven or twelve, my mother
and I were stranded by a broken car deep on a dark
wooded country road. "Don't worry, Mom," I said as
we headed out through pitch black, "I can see with
my feet." She wasn't sure what to make of me, but
she let me lead and we made it out to a neighboring
farmhouse without trouble.

But on this day, on this mountain, I dearly yearned
to follow. I wanted to make my way a small distance
behind our group, in silence. I wanted to be at least a
little alone with the wind and sun and sky. With just
the sound of leaves and birds and this morning's rain-
water trickling along the way. With the low hum of
wise old trees, and the whip of sinewy saplings extend-
ing strong arms along the rocks. My blood sings in
the woods. A song I know in the farthest corners of
my soul. A song I hadn't heard in far too long, and
ached to hear—if only, on this trek, I could follow.

"Let me put my steps in your steps," she said. My
new friend with a new knee and a new hiking pole

and a newfound courage, anxious to put all three to use on a mountain trail this beautiful autumn afternoon. And so, we set off, with her right behind me step for step, others taking the rear behind her, all of us proceeding as quietly as possible.

I'm not exactly sure on what part of the trail it occurred to me that I wasn't leading. At that particularly steep rock outcropping by the reddening maple tree? At the bend where the cottonwoods leaned in to help? The overlook where we all stood breathless, partly because of the view, partly because of the climb? I'm not sure which moment, as I chose my steps with my friend's in mind.

But the thought rose as powerful as my blood rising to muscles that had forgotten all about mountains: "I am following."

AMY CAROL WEBB

WHITE HOUSE

This white house
Made for a white man
Is a symbol of his power
And an aspiration for all white men.
This white house
Was built with black hands.

This white house
That is power through wealth
And wealth with a body count
Is full of ideas to serve a white world.
This white house
Was built with black hands.

This white house
Shelters myths
In a white temple of empire
Where divinity and man's ego converge.
This white house
Was built with black hands.

This white house
Cannot be dismantled
With the master's tool
Because the master's most valuable tool
Built this white house.

ADAM LAWRENCE DYER

WHEN THE UNIMAGINABLE HAPPENED

When we heard the news, saw the wreckage, felt the
    paralyzing blow . . .
our hearts broke open—and spilled out—into our
    hands.

And there we were
watching our Love seep between our fingers,
watching our fragile Love pour out all over us,
watching our Love seem to slip away.

When the unimaginable happened,
the ache that we felt—
as if Love was being lost—
      was the ache of Love's despairing truth.

This is the Love that no one chooses,
the loss so out of order, so profound,
the Love we did not ever want to know.

And yet, the source of this despair,
the reason our hearts cleave and flow,
is because they know fullness.

This is the Love of truth and beauty,
Love that spans the web of being,
uniting each of us within its timeless form.

When we heard the news,
our hearts broke open, spilled into our hands,
and there we stared at Love, lamenting—
    "What am I to do with this?"

And with these raw and tender yearnings
we will—beat after precious beat—
seek wholeness once again.

It will take time to find our balance,
to grieve, if we will make room.
Remember, friends, this is the right thing
    this ache within our deepest beings.
Know that all these things are normal
    to feel disrupted, empty or undone.

Our hearts broke open and the Love that is still true
draws us once again together, story by story, step by
    step,
into places of tender knowing, remembering
to restore us, mend us, piece by broken piece.

This is the Love that runs between us,
sustaining force of restoration,
the Love that nourishes and feeds us,
binds us, each, to our collective core.

We grieve . . . and march . . . and weep . . . and sing
and through the pain—but not despite it—

Love will repair us, not the same, but stronger in
  some places,
    honoring memories like treasures,
    living out our lives' potential
      in the shadow of the trespass
      in the warmth of one another
      in the light of what, restored, we will become.

ANNE BARKER

THE HOLY FAMILY

Writing of the holy family—Mary, Joseph, and the babe Jesus—Wendell Berry once asked what would happen if "we ourselves, opening a stall (a latch thrown open countless times before), might find them breathing there."

I wonder what it would mean for us if we did. If we, still rubbing the sleep from our eyes, with our long daily list of tasks already running through our minds, suddenly stumbled upon the holy family, the holy family right there in front of us, huddled together against the cold, a tiny baby nestled into the arms of his parents?

What would it mean for us to be startled away from our distracted thoughts, pulled suddenly into the intense needs of the moment—warm blankets, soft pillows, hot food? To understand immediately that we would have to make a choice, set aside the list of tasks—the laundry, the child's play date, the stack of papers teetering on the desk—or set aside this . . . this what? This miracle, this wonder, this invitation into another life.

Because we could, of course, set it aside. It wouldn't even be hard, or at least not complicated. We could just turn and walk away, reassure ourselves that someone else would soon come along to help. After all the family is *right there*. We practically fell on top of them, for goodness sake. And honestly, they could be a little more considerate, now that we think about it—move a bit more out of the way instead of acting so entitled, blocking the path of people who are responsible enough to take care of themselves and their own kids. Yeah, someone else will come along soon, not that that family particularly deserves any help.

We could set it aside.

Or . . . we could set the tasks aside. We could allow ourselves to be pulled into the urgency of the moment and then pulled even further, into a world sanctified by joy, by wonder, by the presence of holiness.

We could allow ourselves to be pulled into that sanctified world, with its new mother, luminous and weary from the work of giving birth; with its father, determined and probably a bit afraid; with its babe, intoxicated with the scent of new life, his mouth already opening in hunger. We could choose that world, we could.

I wonder what it would mean for us if we did.

I ask only because I could swear to you that I have been seeing the holy family everywhere: weary mothers, frightened fathers, and hungry children *everywhere.* And maybe you've been seeing them, too. Which would mean that now is the time we have to choose: Do we step around those holy ones on our way to check off our tasks one by one? Or do we step into that other life, with its pressing demands and its astonishing glory, with its refusal to allow us to stumble backwards toward safety and comfort and self-focus?

I ask only because I think they are out there right now, the mothers, the fathers, the children. They are out there and they may be here, waiting. Waiting for us to choose them—waiting for us to feed the hungry, to comfort the weary, to strengthen the frightened, to stand with the weak.

I think they are waiting right now, to see if we will choose rightly.

I wonder what it would mean for us if we did.

JODI COHEN HAYASHIDA

A MEAL, A BED, AND A PHONE CALL

Out of poverty, poetry.
Out of suffering, song.

To the nameless:
We forgive you.

To the broken:
We hear you.

To the mourning and the wandering and the
   invisible:
We see you
As you are

Made from the dust of dew and stars.

We know you
As you are

Super novae and black holes,
Porcelain and beating hearts,
Barbed wire in the early dawn,
A rosary prayed over a desert grave.

DYLAN DEBELIS

ANTIGUA, GUATEMALA

In the eyes of Juana I see reflected
four childbirths, a thousand wash days,
more tortillas baked than stars
peering in the open roof onto her dirt

floor. Sheets of rippled tin shelter beds;
firewood serves to cook, to warm her body.
It is enough, Juana says, for the fifty years
she may live.

A child of privilege, I sit at her splintered
table stuttering across a gulf of culture
in my broken Spanish. We lament
the scarcities of life, celebrate tomorrow

shining in our children's eyes, the coincidence
of time that briefly connects us.
We embrace at the door of this small adobe
house filled with smoke and drying clothes.

SHARON SCHOLL

BENEDICTION FOR THE HEAVY HEART

Good morning. I missed your "good"
because a plane, because a truck, because
a gun, because a cop, because a government,
because a people suffering, because too many
people suffering, because war, because famine,
because some mornings it is so hard
to rise, to wake, to be a self.

There is a pause here. There is a deliberate
cessation. I want a cessation to the noise
in my head, to the ache in the collective
heart of this world. When I was young
this seemed possible. When I was young
how hope seemed to spring eternal.

I want to write about butterflies, about
the cracked edges of tree bark pressing
like a holy mother into palms. I want to write
about the joy of children's cries, about birth,
about the arch of your smile, how I could
lose myself in the corners of your
sweet and grinning mouth. This you is
you reading this. I want for your joy,
want to lose myself in you. I want your
mornings "good," your evenings "good,"
all the late nights and sunrises and afternoons

and moments pressed against the ticking
glass of your life "good."

Breathe. For yourself. For each other. Let
us breathe in when others cannot. When we
can do nothing else. Let us stretch ourselves
open to embrace our friends, extend
our bodies outward to anyone willing to meet us
and even those we think may not be willing. Let us
hold each other for this moment. For this
blink of human existence.

MASON BOLTON

Unitarians and Universalists have been publishing collections of prayers and meditations for more than 175 years. In 1841 the Unitarians broke with their tradition of publishing only formal theology and released *Short Prayers for the Morning and Evening of Every Day in the Week, with Occasional Prayers and Thanksgivings.* Over the ensuing years, the Unitarians published many more volumes of prayers, including Theodore Parker's selections. In 1938, *Gaining a Radiant Faith* by Henry H. Saunderson launched the tradition of an annual Lenten manual.

Several Universalist collections appeared in the early nineteenth century as well. A comprehensive *Book of Prayers* was published in 1839, featuring both public and private devotions. Like the Unitarians, the Universalists published Lenten manuals, and in the 1950s they complemented this series with Advent manuals.

In 1961, the year the Unitarians and Universalists consolidated, the Lenten manual evolved into a meditation manual. And in 2015, reflecting a renewed vision for a wider audience, the name evolved once again into the inSpirit series.

For a complete list of titles in the inSpirit series, please visit **uua.org/inspirit**